The Ark
in the
Garden

Fables for Our Times

The Ark in the Garden

Collected by

Alberto Manguel

Macfarlane Walter & Ross

Toronto

Macfarlane Walter & Ross
37A Hazelton Avenue
Toronto, Canada M5R 2E3

Distributed in Canada by General Distribution Services Ltd.

Distributed in the United States by General Distribution Services Inc.
85 River Rock Drive, Suite 202, Buffalo, New York 14207
Toll-free tel 1-800-805-1083; toll-free fax 1-800-481-6207
e-mail gdsinc@genpub.com

Canadian Cataloguing in Publication Data

Main entry under title:
    The ark in the garden: fables for our times

ISBN 1-55199-030-X

1. Political satire, Canadian (English).* 2. Canadian fiction (English) - 20th century.*
3. Canada – Politics and government – 1993- - Humor.*
I. Manguel, Alberto, 1948- .

PS8375.A74 1998   C813'.5408'0358   C98-932031-6
PR9197.8.A74 1998

Macfarlane Walter & Ross gratefully acknowledges financial support for its publishing program from the Canada Council for the Arts, the Ontario Arts Council, and the Government of Canada through the Book Publishing Industry Development Program.

Printed and bound in Canada

A Christmas Lorac

Margaret Atwood

With profound apologies to Charles Dickens

Ebenezer Scrooge was as good a friend, as good a master, and as good a man as the good old City knew, or the good old Province, or any other good old city, town, borough, or province in the good old world. He gave freely to the poor; his employee, Bob Cratchit, had a Dental Plan, and at Christmas the fattest, jolliest prize Turkey that Scrooge could procure; and to Bob's physically disadvantaged son, Tiny Tim, Scrooge was a second father, and paid into a Provincial Crutch Fund, and supported Wheel-Trans, and swore on his own holly wreath that every penny of it was well spent.

It was the best of times, it was the worst of times. It was the best of times for the Tory Party of Ontario, for their friends and affiliates, and for the big Corporations, which were hauling in record profits; it was the worst of times for just about everyone else. And now it was Christmas! But it was not a very merry one. The spectre of the Deficit haunted men's minds; single mothers rummaged in garbage cans, holding their hollow-cheeked infants by their mittenless hands; battered wives were jeered at by Members of Parliament; beggars bestrewed the streets, crouching in cardboard boxes. Scrooge was troubled, as he made his way homewards through the frosty streets; for he was a good and decent man, and had always paid his share. Where had the ghastly Deficit come from? Was it true that in 1952, individuals had paid 53 percent of all taxes, and now in 1995 they paid 93 percent? Was it true that interest and foreign exchange rates accounted for a whopping 44 percent of the public debt? How then could cutting social programs, a measly 6 percent of expenditures, really help? Something had gone terribly wrong.

In this mood, Scrooge entered his dwelling, noting as he did so that his door-knocker had changed into the head of Ronald Reagan, and was glaring at him. It muttered something about three ghosts, but Scrooge told it that it was just an undigested ham, and it turned back into a door-knocker.

Scrooge's house was dark because he was ecologically conscious, and for the same reason it was cold. He ate his modest supper of Yukon Gold potatoes and Stoney Ridge wine – for Scrooge believed that buying home-grown products was good for the economy – and went to bed.

On the stroke of midnight a dumpy figure clad in silver, with a diamond tiara, stood by his bed. Scrooge thought his Alarm System had malfunctioned – and where were the jolly, round, red little Mounties that were supposed to protect him? But the figure was no earthly being. "I am the Ghost of Christmas Past," she said, "and my name is Maggie. I've come to tell you that you *can* get away with it! Grinding the poor does them good! Makes them step out briskly, spit-spot! And so what if some of them die? Death stiffens the upper lip!"

Scrooge was appalled by these sentiments; but no sooner had this Ghost faded from view than another took its place. It was wearing Day-Glo Alien antennae, and sported a tie covered with alligators. "I am the Ghost of Christmas Present," it said, "and my name is Newt. Here's the big secret – we could fix the Deficit, easy. We could fix the Debt. But we don't want to! The Debt and the Deficit are the best weapons we've ever had, for ruining folks we hate! Come with us, Scrooge! We throw better parties! Why try to help other people? Help yourself, to whatever you can grab! Don't be a fool! Get it while it's going!"

Scrooge found himself wavering. What was the point of being good, when even the leaders were so cold, rapacious, and selfish? Then the third Ghost appeared. It was wearing a veil, and refused to say its name; but one hand was outstretched. Scrooge suspected it was giving him the finger; but, gazing where it pointed, he saw a Province denuded of trees and covered with shopping malls, which were, however, empty, because nobody had jobs any more, and all the rich people had decamped to their condos in Florida. He was the last person in Ontario with employment, and therefore the entire tax burden was now his! What's more, he could no longer walk along the street without being mobbed by ravenous crooks intent on his wallet, and only some of them were politicians.

Scrooge fell to his knees and clutched the Phantom's robe. "Spirit!" he cried. "Pity me! Say that there is at least one more public-minded person left in this Province! Tell me I am not the last!" The Phantom shook its head inexorably. In his agony, Scrooge grasped its hand. He saw an alteration in the Phantom. It shrunk, collapsed, and dwindled into a bedpost.

Yes! And the bedpost was his own. The bed was his own, and the room was his own. Best and happiest of all, the Time was his own, to filch from the needy, just like the leaders of his Province, and to prate about the need to abolish the Deficit, and to add to it by lowering taxes for the middle class, and to call it Common Sense into the bargain!

"My bedpost!" he cried. "Mine, mine, mine! To heck with everyone else!" And he leapt from the bed in his nightshirt, and capered about the room. "I am as light as a forestry stock, that just goes up and up! I am as happy as a big Corporation when it avoids paying taxes! I am as merry as the Tories when they've destroyed all the Arts Organizations, and thus done away with the 11 billion dollars in revenues they generate!"

He got his clothes on somehow, noting that he needed more Gucci shoes, and frisked out onto the street, slicing his cleaning lady's pay in half as he went. "I have seen the error of my ways! Now I'm going to be a squeezing, wrenching, grasping, scraping, clutching, covetous old sinner! And once I've emptied the coffers of this Province, I'm retiring to Florida, to play golf! Whoop! Halloo! You're fired!" he called out gaily to the passers-by.

He skipped along to the home of the Cratchits, where his faithful employee, Bob, and rosy-cheeked Mrs. Cratchit, and all the little Cratchits, including Tiny Tim, were admiring the prize Turkey. "Gimme back that Turkey!" yelped Scrooge. "It's mine! I'm docking your pay, and if you don't like it, you can go on Welfare – except there isn't any Welfare! Hee-hee! I do like a good joke! Oh, and I'm cancelling Wheel-Trans, and repossessing the crutch. It will do Tiny Tim good to become self-reliant! He can learn to walk on his hands!"

"But Tiny Tim can't live on a diet of cracker crumbs and stale bologna!" cried the horrified Cratchits. "Tiny Tim will die!"

"Let him die then," said Scrooge, "and decrease the surplus population."

And Scrooge was as good as his word.

The Ark in the Garden

Timothy Findley

With apologies to James Thurber

Once upon a sunny morning a man sitting in a breakfast nook looked up from his plate to see an ark at the bottom of the garden. He was eating lemon pancakes smothered in maple syrup and melted butter. Rising from the table, he went upstairs to the bedroom, where the drapes had not yet been opened, and spoke to his wife.

"There's an ark in the garden," he said. His napkin was still around his neck.

"Don't be ridiculous," she said. "We burned the last of the ark in the fireplace at New Year's."

"Well, there's another ark."

"Did you make it?"

"No."

"Is your name Noah?"

"Yes."

"Then, unless you made it, there can't be another ark in the garden. Go back down and finish your breakfast."

"But – "

"Go back down and finish your breakfast! I'm going to sleep for another hour."

"Yes, dear."

Noah returned to the breakfast nook, but his heart was sinking. He had lost his appetite. The last ark had landed over twenty centuries before and he himself had been its captain. (People in fables live for a very long time.) On that occasion, Noah had received precise instructions from the Lord regarding the ark's construction – its materials, its size, its design, its capacity, and who was to be let on board. But this time ...

Had the Lord found someone else more trusted and more beloved than Noah?

Well, apparently.

And there the ark sat – in Noah's garden.

The next thing he saw, of course, was a welter of animals trampling his flowers and vegetables. Noah went out beyond the screened porch and approached an elephant who had walked up from the ark and was now standing on the lawn. Noah asked him: "What on earth do you think you're doing?"

The elephant, who was somewhat confused and very sad, said: "I'm doing what all of us are doing. I'm trying to get on board the ark."

"But *why* ... ?" said Noah, with a vague gesture. He meant: *Why is the ark in my garden?* And he also wanted to know: *Why are you walking away from it?*

The elephant thought he meant something else entirely. "Well," he said, "it is what we always do. Whenever things go wrong."

"But nothing's gone wrong!" said Noah, indignant. "I

have just begun to eat the most wonderful stack of lemon pancakes and maple syrup! The sun is shining! Look – you can see it for yourself!"

At that moment, a cloud appeared and blotted out the sun.

Noah wished that his wife had not decided to sleep for another hour. She had a practical side to her reasoning that Noah lacked. He was extremely prone to panic.

"I don't understand," he said to the elephant. "If something's the matter, why aren't you getting on board the ark?"

"I'm not allowed," the elephant said. "And if I were you, I'd go down there at once and apply for admission." The elephant was now on the move again – heading up the hill. "I'm sorry," he called back, "but I don't think I can stay down here any longer."

"Oh, dear," said Noah. "Oh, oh dear ... " And he began to panic.

Noah stared down the hill, where a great many more animals had begun to congregate.

Some years before, Noah had made a rustic lane where the cowpaths had been. It ran between the road up top and the road below, giving Noah access to Sodom, on the one hand, and Gomorrah, on the other. Not that Noah ever went to visit these cities – but he did have goods delivered which could be ordered by phone: birdseed and cow bran, binder-twine and calf-pullers. Now he could see that the gates at either end of his lane had apparently been opened and a stream of animals, motorcars, and even excursion buses was pouring through from each direction.

Still with his napkin tied round his neck, he loped halfway down the hill. But so many animals were coming up – animals, trucks, and even busloads of people – that he could not make his way.

"What's happening?" he called out several times, and at last a gnu who had bruised her knees took time to pause and tell him.

"There's a man down there," she said, "who has a List. And only those on The List are allowed on board."

"What man? What man?"

"I couldn't make out his name," said the gnu, "but his List includes a great many jaguars and ... and ... like that. No gnus at all. In fact, the only animals I've seen going aboard are fatted calves and guinea fowl. It has to make a person very suspicious."

"Indeed," said Noah.

"I must make for higher ground," said the gnu. "I hope you will forgive me, but I'm lame."

"Go right ahead," said Noah. "Dear, dear. Oh, dear, dear!"

From behind him, and passing to his left, a large flotilla of motorcars appeared. The first in line were the Jaguars.

"Jaguars," Noah muttered. "The gnu said Jaguars were allowed on board."

And behind them came all the other motorcars – two by two.

"Millionaires!" Noah sputtered. "In their millionaire cars!"

Mercedeses, Daimlers, and Rolls-Royces, Cadillacs, Range Rovers, and Lincolns rolled through the dust down the lane. All had tinted windows. The passengers could not be seen.

At the lower gate, beyond which the ark loomed up as if from memory, Noah found and accosted the man with The List. He wore sunglasses.

"Is my name on there?" Noah asked.

"Depends what it is."

Noah told him.

The man, who also wore gloves, ran his fingers through the N's.

"Nope," he said. "Not here."

"But – ! I'm *Noah!*"

"Do you have a Jaguar?"

"No. I have farm animals – horses ... sheep ..."

"Not good enough. Go back."

Taking one last look at the chaotic scene before him, Noah sighed and joined the growing crowd of refugees moving up the hill away from the ark – and, where the path diverged to his side door, returned to his kitchen.

There sat his wife, finishing his pancakes.

"Well?" she said. "What's going on out there?"

Noah told about the ark and all the millionaires' cars, the elephant and the gnu. Then he took off his napkin and wiped his brow.

"I suppose in that case we'd best get going," said his wife, with a dab at her lips and a final mouthful of coffee.

"No," said Noah. "No need to hurry. We aren't going anywhere."

"Not going anywhere? But we have to get on board the ark!"

"No," said Noah – and sat down. "Not this time." Then he said: "There's a man with a List – and we're not on it."

"But this is Canada! Our home and native land! We're on every list there is! Old age pensions – after all, nobody's older than we are! And what about – health care ... ark privileges ... They can't sail without us!"

"Well, they're going to," said Noah. "And there's nothing we can do about it. Are there any more pancakes?"

"No."

It began to rain.

Moral: No gnus is bad gnus. In other words, if you want to survive today – you had best get on the right list.

Come, Said the Eagle

Neil Bissoondath

Come, said the Eagle,
Come, let's eat,
From this Maple tree
Oh, so sweet!

As dawn breaks, the farmer's wife sinks heavily into a kitchen chair. She has been up for hours labouring to prepare breakfast and lunch for her large family and now she is exhausted.

Her husband and all their eight sons are already out in the fields digging and plowing, preparing the earth for seed. The house is empty save for her and her husband's father, who lives with them and who is, as always, taking his breakfast alone at his table in a corner of the kitchen. Her husband doesn't understand his father's wish to eat alone, but she knows that her father-in-law has secured for himself the warmest spot in the house, right beside the stove.

She is hungry, and as she bites into her slice of buttered bread, she hears Grandfather say, "You know, Daughter-in-Law, it is not a bad life you have. My son loves you, my grandsons love you. Why, even I ... Our farm is the envy of the region. No, not a bad life at all."

"I know, Grandfather," she says, sipping at her coffee long grown cold.

"Why then do you continue to dream of another life?"

"How do you know I continue to dream of another life?"

"I see it in your eyes, I hear it in your footsteps. It is as if some far-off voice is calling to you."

She takes another bite of bread. Yes, she thinks, that is it exactly.

No, said the Beaver,
Not today,
This tree's all mine –
Yours? No way!

Grandfather says, "You cannot leave, Daughter-in-Law. You have responsibilities. You must help my son and me keep this family together. If we fail in our duty, all that we have worked so hard for will be gone, swallowed up by the neighbours who have long coveted our springs, our rich fields, and our maple groves." He pauses, his voice gravelly with a cough. "Family is everything, Daughter-in-Law, surely you must know that."

She finishes off the bread, takes a last sip of coffee, and sets about washing up the pile of dirty dishes.

Grandfather, watching her, says, "My son needs you. He

does not know it, or perhaps he does not have the words to tell you. But he needs you."

He needs me? she thinks. Once, perhaps, he did. And once, perhaps, he understood. But that has not been so for some time.

"And your elder sons need you. They do not know you well – "

Who does? she wonders.

" – but love you they do, even if they do not understand your needs."

Who does? she wonders again.

"Without you, they would not know themselves."

But they, too, are discontented, she thinks, though their reasons be different. They feel ignored, and isolated, and unimportant. They feel that they, too, must have a voice in the decisions of the family: on what should be sown, when and where, on how the crop should be divided up. But this, they feel, they have been denied.

Hold on, said the Otter,
All yours, says who?
It's yours and mine
And everyone else's too!

"And your younger sons need you. What will happen to them without you to support them against the older ones, who are so much more powerful than they? All this squabbling over the land. Without you, it's the poorhouse for them."

At the mention of the younger ones, her heart softens. Yes, they are the weaklings of the family, not in soul but in body. It is in them that she most sees herself: decent and hard-working, wishing always for the best but undone by the others. She does all she can for them, but of what use will she be if she is herself undone?

"You are the only woman in this family. Yours are tastes unique among the women of the region. You make us special. You make us what we are. Without you, we cannot hold."

She looks at her reflection in the window above the sink.

She is no longer young, but she is pretty still and feels within herself the energy and strength with which she could yet create for herself a new life.

A new life! How long she has dreamt of that. How tempting it remains.

Twice in the past she has steeled herself to take the step.

The first time, as she came down the stairs with her suitcase, Grandfather shouted at her: "You will leave here with nothing! You will end up penniless in the streets!" And then, seeing threats to be of no avail, he made promises: of help with the housework; of time to pursue her own interests. Halfway across the living room, she turned around.

But those promises were never kept. Her sons had resisted.

Now see here, said Bear,
I want my own,
With branches and leaves
to call my home.

The second time, she made it to the door, despite the cries of her family, their protestations of love. And as she stood on the very threshold, her nerve failed her. Again there were promises of change, but her family, seeing her retreat for the second time, quickly forgot. They had other, more pressing concerns: the pigsties to be cleaned out, the horses to be reshod.

She dries the dishes and puts them into the cupboards.

Grandfather, no longer young but vigorous still, rises from the table, wipes his lips, and tosses the napkin to the floor. "I must go inspect the fences now," he says. "But we will talk again later, Daughter-in-Law."

To what purpose? she wonders.

As she clears the dishes from Grandfather's table, she thinks of the disdain in which her family holds her needs. They are happy with their lot, and cannot understand why she should require time to read the books that stir her, to listen to the music that moves her, and above all to scribble her silly verses.

We, too, work hard all day, they said. Why should you be different?

Because I am, she replied. Are you blind?

But they were blind: If you have free time, they said, then so too must we all – and that is not possible.

She unties her apron and folds it over the back of a chair. Then she goes up to the bedroom, straightens her hair, removes her ring, and reaches under the bed for the suitcase she has never unpacked.

She walks down the stairs, across the living room, opens the door, and steps outside. The morning sun is warm on her skin, yet she feels herself shiver: with fear, with anticipation. Part of her does not wish to do this, but she knows that leaving is now her only possibility.

As she sets off down the gravel road that leads away from the house, away from the farm, she remembers that she has left Grandfather's napkin lying on the floor.

She smiles: So be it, then.

High above in the clear, blue sky a circling eagle screeches in farewell.

Go on, said the Eagle,
Squabble for me.
I've always wanted
my very own Maple tree.

The Axe and the Trees

Jane Urquhart

Once upon a time in a remote part of a northern land there lived a large extended family of wise old trees. Solid, proud, and strong, their foliage forever green, they had existed for hundreds of years in perfect harmony with the forest life around them. They had provided shade and cover for many sleek, soft-footed animals. They had provided homes for the many-coloured birds who sent the world's most beautiful music up to heaven from the branches. And occasionally they would generously drop one or two of their many limbs down to the ground so that the community of human beings who dwelt nearby might have chairs to sit upon and tables to eat at, and, in the winter, bright coals to warm their hands by.

The human beings loved the trees, knowing that their lives would be neither comfortable nor complete without them. They loved the heat they gave them in the winter, and the useful things that were made from their wood, but most of all they loved the way the trees looked in the slanting light of early morning or evening, or how they glistened after the rain. Often the human beings would walk among the trees, pausing now and then to touch the grainy trunks or to look up from the forest floor at the ceiling of green branches high above them. All the songs these people sang were hymns of praise to the trees.

Then, one day, into the forest there swaggered a bright young axe from the south who announced that he must cut down a great number of the trees for his bosses who lived in cities where wood was no longer plentiful. The people argued with him. They told him he could take pine cones with him to the south, where they would grow into similar large wonderful trees who would generously drop a limb or two to the ground which could be used for tables or chairs or to warm one's hands by. But the axe said that neither he nor his bosses had any time for this, that somebody else's bosses had promised a great deal of money for the trees, and that money waits for neither man nor axe. The trees argued with him too. Your head is made of cold, hard steel, they told him, but your heart is just like ours, it being made of the warm flesh of wood. Surely in your heart you do not want to cut us down. The axe replied that he did not think with his heart, and that his heart was incapable of adding up the large sums of money his bosses would get from the trees. Furthermore, he said to the trees, this is what I do for a living. If I don't cut you down I will have no other form of employment. I'm not like your hippie friends over there, loafing around in forests, looking at trees and making up those ridiculous hymns of praise. I'm going to do something with my life, I'm going to make a lot of money for my bosses. And with that he set to work.

In the weeks and months that followed, the people's hymns of praise were drowned out by the noise of the axe striking the flesh of the trees and the sound of the trees themselves groaning as they fell to the forest floor. It wasn't long before the people stopped singing altogether, and then it wasn't much longer after that that the people began to die of sorrow from listening to the sound of their friends the trees being murdered by the axe.

Eventually, the axe was all alone, his head on fire from the bright sun (there was no shade) and his wooden handle weak and thin from overwork. Every day messages arrived from his bosses in the south. We need more wood, they said, we haven't got enough money yet. This forest is all gone, the axe replied, I've cut it all down. Well, then, find another forest, shouted the bosses from the south, and find it fast or we will send a chainsaw up there to replace you.

Dispiritedly the axe set off in search of another forest, but everywhere he went he found emptiness and desolation, for other axes had been there before him. He sent a message to his bosses in the south. I need some money, it read, my varnish is all worn off and my head is coming loose. What makes you think that taxpayers should pay for your maintenance, the bosses responded, and furthermore, all money belongs to us. Remember?

Then one day the axe's wooden handle broke in half and fell away from his hard steel head.

Oh no! the axe cried. I am utterly useless, I cannot exist without my handle. I must have a new handle, otherwise I'm finished. An axe is nothing without a handle. He looked around him desperately, but, of course, there was no wood to be seen and even had there been the odd scrap left behind, there were no human beings to make useful things out of it.

I need a new handle, the axe shouted. But, of course, no one heard him.

Moral: Even if you have a head of hard cold steel, it is prudent to remember that your handle is of wood.

FIG. 82. Perfect functional and anatomical results six weeks after operation. Note extension. (Courtesy of Institute of Golf Anatomy).

From Plus-Fours to Minus-Fours

Rohinton Mistry

There are two songs from two musicals of the sixties whose inspirational lyrics might recommend them for an occasion such as this: "Let's Go Fly a Kite" from *Mary Poppins* and "Climb Every Mountain" from *The Sound of Music*. Now it would be grand if the times were such that these two songs – replete with their avian metaphors and energetic images of soaring kites, their exhortations to climb rainbow-swathed alpine peaks and plunge into ice-cold mountain streams – could present us with a full and complete philosophy of life. Unfortunately, the times are not such, and

I'm not sure if there ever was a time when the times were such. And so I've had to write a little fable, to complement the two songs.

Once upon a time, not so very long ago, in a land that was not at all far away, there lived a people who were considered the most fortunate by the rest of the world. And there was good reason for this: theirs was a land that was blessed in every way. But, what was more significant, theirs was a society that lived by the principles of tolerance and good will and compassion for its members. Now, not all of the citizens were bursting with tolerance and good will and compassion all of the time, but the important thing was: they did their best to *believe* in these values, they believed they were worth striving after.

The people of this fortunate land had two passions: kite-flying and mountain-climbing. Some practised one, some the other; many practised both. The most accomplished among them flew their kites from the mountain tops, and it was a truly awe-inspiring sight. The kite-flyers and mountain-climbers had their various teams, the team uniforms were fashioned in fabrics of red and white, and they took great pleasure in friendly competitions and games. But they never forgot their credo of tolerance and good will and compassion.

Thus, they were always urging the less agile among them to climb the mountains, and assisting those who had not yet mastered the laws of aerodynamics and glue and paper to fly their kites. Special agencies had even been set up to bring to fruition this vision of a just society. And so the disabled, the feeble, those too poor to buy their mountain-climbing gear or their kite-flying equipment and, most important, their elegant red-and-white uniforms were all looked after and encouraged to participate fully.

The wise king of this fortunate land, himself an enthusiast of kites and mountains like his predecessors, gazed upon his kingdom and saw that it was good. He watched his people singing and laughing and playing together, and his eyes moistened with happiness.

Now it came to pass that there arose in the land a shortage of cloth. No one could explain exactly why the shortage arose, especially in such a prosperous land, but it had something to do with people who called themselves international fabric-traders, who speculated in the commodity and created artificial deficits. The good king did his best to ensure that his people would not suffer. He lowered tariffs, raised taxes, tried to impose rules and regulations on the traders, but in the end the fabricated deficits defeated him. The scarcity of cloth made him take the unprecedented step of establishing limits on people's wardrobes.

Most people accepted this modest restriction. They understood that it was fair, equitable, and necessary for the common good. But there were some who protested, especially when their cherished red-and-white team uniforms were unavailable. The dissent spread and, as is inevitable in these situations, brought forth in their midst a challenger who promised he could restore prosperity to the land if he became king.

"Waste in the king's bureaucracy is the reason for this shortage," he said. "I will cut out the waste. I will downsize and restructure and consolidate. I will be lean and mean for a while, but soon you will reap the rewards, trust me."

This is what he said in public. In private, he would stand before his full-length mirror and sing a different song: "Oh-uh-oh yes, I'm the great pretender."

In view of his healthy girth, the need for leanness was self-evident, but why meanness? Alas, no one sought to question him on this point, and then he was already ensconced on the throne of the realm.

The new measures now went into effect. The first proclamation stated that no more fabric would be issued from the royal textile warehouses for uniforms for kite-flyers and mountain-climbers. The new king had no interest in these two groups – he himself was a golfer. Meanwhile, red, white, *and* blue fabric continued to be made available for golf shirts and golf slacks and plus-fours.

The unfairness of it all was not lost on the people. When

they complained, the new king said: "Golf is the activity of the nineties. It's a now kind of thing, a global thing. It will bring prosperity to the land, and soon there'll be fabric enough for everyone. It's the theory of trickle-down textiles."

Time passed, but balls – stray golf balls – were all that trickled down the courses. Sometimes they flew at great speed, injuring innocent bystanders. In retaliation, groups of kite-flyers and mountain-climbers began attacking golfers, tearing their clothes off, altering their plus-fours to minus-fours. It became necessary for the king to station his imperial guard on every fairway and green. With their black face visors, body armour, and weapons, the guards looked as though they had stepped out of a video game rife with unspeakable violence.

The shortage of fabric in the land did not abate. The king went on television and explained that further austerity measures were needed before things could get better. "We have no choice but to issue a downsizing decree," he said. "We are not mean-spirited or heartless, as some of our enemies suggest. We do not enjoy causing pain. But we have to fulfil our promises." Between sentences, the king's lips kept disappearing; he continued: "We will start by saving on skirts and trousers. People's legs will be downsized. Less fabric will then be required to clothe them. Instead of the ankle bone connecting to the leg bone, the leg bone connecting to the knee bone, the knee bone to the thigh bone, and the thigh bone to the hip bone, we will eliminate all the surplus and connect the ankle bone directly to the hip bone. Then everyone can wear very short pants and very short skirts. The savings will be immense."

The first cuts began to take effect, and the cries of the people rent the once-tranquil air of the land. The kite-flyers and mountain-climbers pleaded that such drastic measures were not necessary; there were surely better ways to deal with the cloth shortage.

"We can't be distracted by special-interest groups," said the king.

"But Sire, we will no longer be able to fly our kites and

climb the beautiful mountains," said the people.

"Nonsense," said the king, unable to control what seemed to be a tiny smirk. "Of course you will. It will be a greater challenge, that's all. Your downsized legs will have to work harder, that's all. My daddy taught me that if I worked hard, I would be able to fly kites and climb mountains as much as I wanted."

As the cutbacks continued, the king noticed that things were not proceeding fast enough. He inquired into the delays. The surgeons in charge of downsizing legs said, "We do not have enough operating theatres and hospital beds."

"Is that all?" said the king. He met with his advisors. A new decree went forth: the butchers and meat-packers and all the abattoirs in the land were to pitch in. "Same difference," said the king. "They all work with flesh and bone, and use the same tools. We have too much specialization for our own good." He wiped his sweat-beaded upper lip and continued. "While we are at it, let us restructure education. From now on, metal workshop teachers will also teach English – they can recite a sonnet, for example, while giving a welding demonstration. And the English teachers will be retrained as caddies – they'll be more useful on our golf courses."

Misery and despair settled like a fog upon the land. And the people saw that once again the golfers were left unscathed. In fact, the golfers seemed to *grow* in size. The amputated leg bones and thigh bones were being grafted onto the golfers, making them taller and stronger than ever before. Now they were able to stride faster down the fairways, sinking holes-in-one with regularity, completing their eighteen holes in no time.

The kite-flyers and mountain-climbers, their numbers greatly dwindled, crawled to the king in their very short pants and very short skirts and tried to explain that it was not just a luxury or a hobby of which they were being deprived. "All of society suffers, Your Highness, downsizing diminishes us all, including Your Majesty and the members of your royal court."

"And how's that?" asked the king, standing tall.

"Kite-flying and mountain-climbing are necessary for our spiritual well-being," said the people. "Kites let you soar as though you had your own set of wings. Your feet stay grounded but you're in flight, so long as you hold tight to the string of your kite."

"Rhyming rubbish and figurative flim-flam," said the king dismissively.

"But, Sire, from the mountain top you can see forever, it's like having a glimpse of the paradise that we could share on earth. Kites and mountains – they help us to dream. And you are taking away our dreams, Your Majesty. Without dreams, people perish. Come with us, fly a kite with us, hike up to the mountain top with us. Even a small, teensy-weensy mountain will enrich you."

"Socialist claptrap and metaphorical mumbo-jumbo cannot shake my belief in common sense," declared the king, his lips disappearing completely as he spoke.

And like the king's lips, the art of kite-flying and mountain-climbing also disappeared from people's lives with the passing of time. But it lived on in their hearts and minds, and in their imagination. It helped them to endure, it kept hope alive, for they continued to secretly sing their two songs while waiting for deliverance.

The Banana Wars

Yves Beauchemin

Translated by Alberto Manguel

Towards the end of a sunny afternoon, the tribe of Long Hand monkeys in the Land of Gallinaco was attacked by the tribe of Big Foot monkeys of the Island of Felido, from where they had furtively arrived on balsa rafts. A brief battle took place, sticks and stones flew through the air, blood was shed, and the Long Hand monkeys, outnumbered, suffered a bitter defeat.

"From now on, this land is ours," the Big Foot general announced to the chief of the defeated Long Hand. "We will make it our country. Out of sheer kindness, we will allow you to live on here, but you shall have to abide by our rules."

"That seems fair," answered the chief, bowing his head. "We accept."

The Long Hand monkeys lost their right to climb the banana trees to pick bananas. This became the exclusive right of the Big Foot monkeys, who decided to make bananas their staple trade. They ate as many bananas as they liked, they dried the surplus to sell it abroad, and they gave the banana skins to the Long Hand monkeys in exchange for their labour.

"We don't like banana skins," the Long Hand monkeys complained. "They taste too bitter. We always used to eat the flesh."

"Those days are now gone," was the answer. "From now on, you are to eat the skins. Perhaps it's true that the skins are a trifle bitter, but they are nourishing. We envy you."

A few months went by. The Long Hand monkeys wandered through the jungle, weak, downcast, and uneasy. From time to time, one of them would meet a Big Foot monkey, and they would exchange angry bites.

"If things go on like this," the defeated Long Hand moaned, "our children will have forgotten how to climb the banana trees in search of food and then they will no longer be true monkeys."

It became necessary to post a Big Foot monkey armed with a stone in front of every banana tree, because under cover of night, bananas were being stolen. As there were not enough guards, Long Hand monkeys were recruited to fill the gaps; as a reward for their services, they were given the right to eat a banana, from time to time and in secret. The Long Hand thus recruited felt deeply satisfied and wonderfully important.

The two tribes shared the same territory but lived apart, spying at one another among the trees and the ferns. Gallinaco, once so joyful and bustling, was now enveloped in a melancholic atmosphere, even on sunny days.

One night, Lojo, chief of the Long Hand monkeys, assembled some twenty of his tribe and attacked the invaders in an attempt to chase them away. After a long and noisy battle, the Long Hand monkeys were defeated for the second time; their chief was hit on the head with a coconut and was no longer able to lead them.

"Thank God," sighed the Big Foot monkeys. "At last we'll enjoy some peace."

But their relief did not last long. The atmosphere at Gallinaco became grimmer and grimmer, and the skirmishes increased and became sneakier and crueller.

The Long Hand monkeys elected in secret another chief, Bobo, and he chose the cleverest members of the tribe to try to find a way of improving their common lot.

"We need to compromise," they concluded unanimously.

The next day, Bobo sought out Zoyo, chief of the Big Foot monkeys, and said to him the following:

"Allow us to climb only ten of the banana trees. This will allow us to have just a taste of the bananas and thus lighten our sorrow. In exchange, I promise you peace."

"I'll think about it," Zoyo answered.

He called his counsellors to him and asked for their opinion.

"An excellent idea," they answered. "To climb some ten banana trees will give them the illusion of climbing all banana trees. Furthermore, they are bound to quarrel over their share of bananas. And during that time, we shall have peace."

Zoyo summoned Bobo and ten banana trees were adorned with a white flower; the Long Hand monkeys were given permission to climb those trees and pick bananas for themselves.

A certain joyfulness returned for a time to Gallinaco, but very soon squabbling broke out, because everyone wanted a taste of banana, but there were not enough bananas to go around.

So Bobo returned to Zoyo and asked for ten more banana trees.

"With ten more banana trees, everyone will be happy, and peace will reign forever in Gallinaco."

But Zoyo refused point blank and summoned once again his counsellors.

"You gave me the wrong advice," he blamed them. "Now we've encouraged their taste for bananas when what we should have done was quench it for ever. Do not repeat this mistake, or you will be eating banana peels yourself."

"From now," they said contritely, "we will endeavour to show better judgment."

But things went from bad to worse in Gallinaco. Among the Long Hand monkeys, certain unscrupulous individuals set up a black market in bananas. Dissatisfaction grew. The quarrels multiplied. And rather than diminish, the Long Hand's dislike for their masters seemed to increase ever more.

Bobo's prestige declined daily among his own people. That of Zoyo likewise, since the Big Foot's future appeared gloomier and gloomier.

Then all of a sudden, Fino, one of the cleverest of the Long Hand monkeys, called the tribe together, saying that he had a plan he wanted to put forward.

"Bobo, our chief, needs to take a rest. While he gathers

his strength once more, I would be willing to take his place. I have an idea to suggest that might better our lot."

"What idea is that?" they asked.

"I want to become your leader, but I also will become the leader of the Big Foot. In that way, we will no longer suffer ill treatment from anyone, since I will have become everyone's protector and a cordial understanding will reign throughout the land."

His words were greeted with a roar of laughter.

"You who are so clever, how can you speak such nonsense?" asked an old monkey between hiccups. "Perhaps you got hit on the head with a coconut!"

"Nothing hit me on the head," was Fino's stern reply. "Let me go meet with the Big Foot. If I do not succeed in convincing them, you may laugh at me as much as you wish."

There was a lengthy discussion and at last an elder rose to his feet and said:

"Fino has always had bright ideas. Let us give him a chance."

"Let us give him a chance!" the crowd echoed.

So Fino was sent to parley with the Big Foot. He asked Zoyo, their chief, to call them together and he spoke to them thus:

"Hatred between our tribes keeps growing. If we do nothing about it, war will break out once again. Perhaps you will win as before, perhaps not. Who indeed can see into the future? Elect me as your leader. My tribe has chosen me already. I promise I will keep them calm and obedient, because they trust me. And in that way you will be able to conduct your business in peace and quiet."

Zoyo tried to oppose him, but the Big Foot monkeys found Fino's idea so ingenious that they deposed their leader there and then, and named Fino in his place.

For several months peace reigned in Gallinaco. Never before had one monkey been the leader of both tribes simultaneously! Admirers came from everywhere to congratulate him and to try to understand how he had managed to pull off such a stunt. And Fino kept a modest profile, but his victory was quickly rising to his head.

And yet, the lot of the Long Hand monkeys had scarcely improved. They still had only ten banana trees at their disposal and most of them had to feed on banana peels all year long.

Fino tried to satisfy the interests of both tribes. But since the Big Foot monkeys were far more numerous than the Long Hand monkeys, the spirit of justice forced him, more often than not, to lean in favour of the former.

Grumblings began to be heard among the vanquished. Certain Long Hand monkeys spoke of treason. So Fino convinced the Big Foot tribe to give the Long Hand tribe two more banana trees. The handing-over took place during a sumptuous ceremony. Drums were beaten under a shower of white flowers. Everyone rejoiced.

At the end of the day, Fino summoned several elders of the Long Hand tribe and announced to them, after they had been sworn to secrecy, that this handing-over was only the beginning and that there would be many others. With a little patience, he said, they would in the end recover practically all their lost banana trees. Then he summoned several elders of the Big Foot tribe and told them that, for the sake of peace, he would be forced, from time to time, to hand over to the vanquished a few more banana trees, but that these would be few and far between, so as not to damage business in any way.

A year passed. Fino's fame spread far beyond Gallinaco and all over the jungle. Now, when he strolled among his subjects, Fino would drop all appearance of modesty and strut around with an insolent swagger. No one dared address him except in respectful tones and after long reflection, since he no longer accepted any criticism. And yet, he lost none of his perspicacity and sensed that a secret revolution was simmering among the Long Hand monkeys. One evening, a spy entered his cabin and told him that a revolt was in the making.

Fino ordered that the troublemakers be arrested at once, and assembled his counsellors. The discussion was long and loud. Finally, one of the counsellors had a simple but remarkable idea.

"What matters most to the Long Hand monkeys," he said, "is not the actual eating of bananas but *climbing up the banana trees*. Therefore, let us allow them to climb up all the banana trees that we have already picked bare, and they will be under the impression of having found almost all their old freedom once again."

Fino, with a big grin on his face, nodded his head.

"An excellent idea. We will call those banana trees *distinct* banana trees, and only the Long Hand monkeys will be allowed to climb them. That will no doubt cause jealousy among the Big Foot monkeys, but their jealousy will be dear to us."

Everyone clapped.

Fino called the meeting to an end and went to bed smiling, certain that he had brought peace to the land for ever and ever more.

This book has been typeset in
DaddyO, Gill Sans and New Century Schoolbook.

The illustrations are by:

Barry Blitt

A Christmas Lorac

Shelagh Armstrong-Hodgson

The Ark in the Garden

Jeff Jackson

Come, Said the Eagle

Jamie Bennett

The Axe and the Trees

Gary Clement

From Plus-Fours to Minus-Fours

Sandra Dionisi

The Banana Wars

Book design by:

Spencer Francey Peters